WITHDRAWN

Artists Through the Ages

Leonardo da Vinci

Alix Wood

WINDMILL BOOKS

New York

Published in 2013 by Windmill Books, An Imprint of Rosen Publishing
29 East 21st Street, New York, NY 10010

Editor for Alix Wood Books: Eloise Macgregor
US Editor: Sara Antill
Designer: Alix Wood

Photo Credits: Cover, 1 © Alinari - Artothek; 6 © Artothek; 7 © Paolo Tosi -
Artothek; 9 © Peter Willi - Artothek; 10 © Christie's Images Ltd - Artothek; 11
© Michael Reed; 13 bottom © Léonard de Serres, Château du Clos Lucé; 17 ©
Peter Willi - Artothek; 22 © Sheila Terry/Science Photo Library, 23 © brandonht
- Shutterstock; 24-25 © Artothek; 26 © Alinari - Artothek; 29 © Musée de la Ville
de Paris, Musée du Petit-Palais, France/The Bridgeman Art Library; 3, 4 top and
bottom, 5, 12, 13 top and center, 15, 18, 19, 20, 21, 22, 27, 28 © Shutterstock

Library of Congress Cataloging-in-Publication Data

Wood, Alix.
 Leonardo da Vinci / by Alix Wood.
    p. cm. — (Artists through the ages)
 Includes index.
 ISBN 978-1-61533-621-0 (library binding) — ISBN 978-1-61533-629-6 (pbk.)
 — ISBN 978-1-61533-630-2 (6-pack)
 1. Leonardo, da Vinci, 1452–1519—Juvenile literature. 2. Artists—Italy—
Biography—Juvenile literature. I. Title.
 N6923.L33W66 2013
 709.2—dc23
 [B]

                               2012025841

Manufactured in the United States of America

CPSIA Compliance Information: Batch #BW13WM: For Further Information contact Windmill Books, New York, New York at 1-866-478-0556

Contents

Who Was Leonardo?

An engraving of Leonardo by J. Posselwhite

Leonardo da Vinci was a painter, sculptor, engineer, mathematician, philosopher, and architect! His name means "Leonardo from Vinci" but he may have been born in Anchiano, near Vinci, in Italy. His father was a lawyer, and his mother was a peasant woman. They never married. Leonardo lived most of his childhood with his father and stepmother, Albiera.

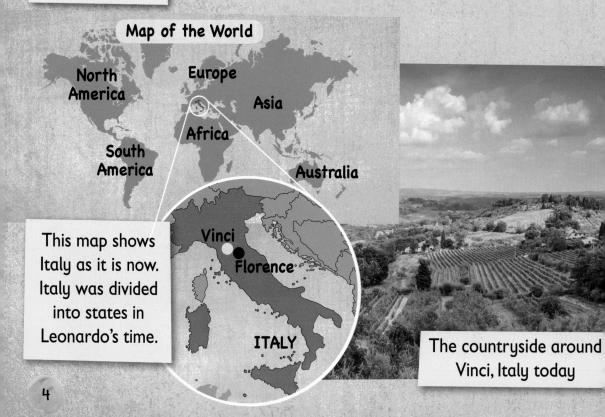

Map of the World

North America

Europe

Asia

Africa

South America

Australia

Vinci

Florence

ITALY

This map shows Italy as it is now. Italy was divided into states in Leonardo's time.

The countryside around Vinci, Italy today

Leonardo's early education was probably organized by his stepmother and grandmother. He showed a talent for drawing and design. At 14, Leonardo's father recognized what great talent he had with painting. Leonardo had painted a dragon that looked so real that it actually scared his father! Father and son went to Florence, and Leonardo became an **apprentice** to one of the leading artists in the city, Andrea di Cione, called Verrocchio, which means "true eye."

The Renaissance

"Renaissance" means "rebirth." The Renaissance period began around 1350 in Italy, and continued until about 1600. It was a time of creativity, imagination, and curiosity. New ideas in art, science, astronomy, religion, literature, math, philosophy, and politics were developed. It was also an age of exploration. The invention of the printing press in 1450 meant new ideas could spread with printed books.

A statue of Leonardo da Vinci outside the Uffizi Gallery, in Florence

LEONARDO DA VINCI

5

Learning to Paint

At Verrocchio's **studio**, Leonardo showed how great an artist he was going to become. He helped paint Verrocchio's *Baptism of Christ,* shown on the right. Leonardo painted the left-hand angel and some of the background. Leonardo's addition and several other "corrections" were done using a form of oil paint, even though Verrocchio began this piece using **tempera**! Leonardo wanted the effects possible from oil paint, such as transparent and glowing skin, shining jewelry, and silky hair.

Several Verrocchio paintings are thought to be by Leonardo. *The Annunciation,* above, has Verrocchio's style, but the composition and atmosphere are like paintings by Leonardo.

Baptism of Christ. Verrocchio was apparently so affected by his pupil's skillful work painting the angel that he never painted again!

Missing Deadlines

After leaving Verrocchio's studio, Leonardo gained a **reputation** for not delivering work on time. *The Adoration of the Magi* for the monks at San Donato a Scopeto in Florence, was left unfinished when Leonardo left Florence for Milan. The work was finished by another artist. In Milan in 1483, Leonardo received another important commission from the Church of San Francesco Grande. *The Virgin of the Rocks* was to be finished in seven months, but wasn't delivered for another 25 years!

The Virgin of the Rocks

Ten years into the seven month project there was an argument about money. Leonardo wanted payment for the expensive frame he had bought. The church refused and sued him for not finishing the painting on time. Leonardo sold the painting to someone else around 1491. When the argument was settled Leonardo started working on a new version for the church. He delivered it, unfinished, in 1499, and then finished it a year or so later!

The Virgin of the Rocks. This is the first version of the painting.

The *Great Horse*

In 1482 Leonardo wrote a letter to the ruler of Milan, Duke Ludovico Sforza. He recommended himself as a military inventor and engineer. Leonardo's letter earned him a commission from Sforza and in 1483 he began work on a sculpture, the *Great Horse*.

Leonardo was to create a huge horse about 24 feet (7.3 m) high. Such a task had never been done before. A full-sized clay model was finished in 1493. To finish the horse, tons (t) of bronze were needed. However, Sforza used the bronze to make weapons and Leonardo's work was never completed.

One of Leonardo's horse sketches

When the French took Milan in 1499, the giant clay horse was used as target practice by French archers! The sketches that Leonardo made survived, though. Years later, a retired American pilot, Charles Dent, became fascinated by the story of the bronze horse. He decided to try and finish the sculpture.

Cast at Last

In 1999, two 24-foot-(7.3 m) tall bronze statues by Nina Akamu were unveiled in Milan, Italy, and Grand Rapids, Michigan.

Leonardo's Horse, Grand Rapids, Michigan

Military Engineer

Leonardo was fascinated by technology and the workings of machines. Hundreds of inventions were sketched out in his notebooks. In his letter to Duke Ludovico Sforza, Leonardo had written that he could construct bridges which were light and strong and portable. He also said he could make a kind of cannon which was light, easy to transport, and could hurl small stones like hail.

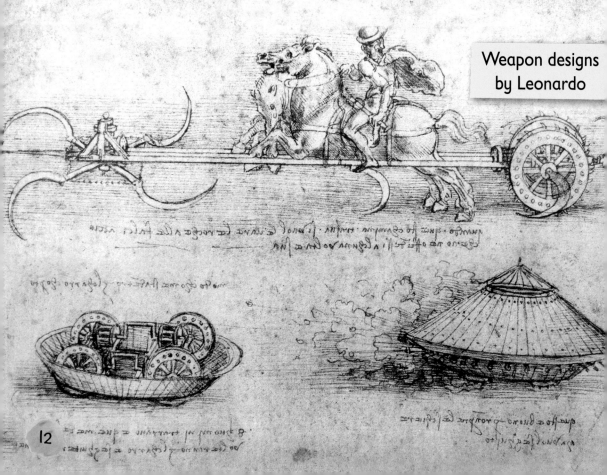

Weapon designs by Leonardo

While working for Ludovico Sforza, Leonardo designed his ultimate war machine, an armored tank. Driven by the muscle power of eight men, the tank was a turtle-like moving shell with 36 guns. The eight men would have been protected by the outer shell, so they could have driven the tank at walking speed right into the heat of battle unharmed. The guns, firing in all directions, would have been terrifying.

Model of the tank in the Clos Lucé garden, in France, made from Leonardo's drawings

Deliberate Mistake?

There is a flaw in Leonardo's tank design. The gears make the front wheels move in the opposite direction to the rear wheels. The tank would have been unable to move! Leonardo was too clever to make a mistake like that. Historians believe he either didn't want the tank to be made, or he was afraid that his diagram would fall into enemy hands. He made the error to make sure nobody could build the tank but him.

13

Mirror Writing

Mirror writing is writing completely back to front, so you start each line from the right side of the page, and turn each letter around so it's backward. You can only read what you have written with a mirror.

ϱnitiɿw ɿoɿɿim ƨi ƨidT

Can you read the words on the left? Hold a mirror here.

Leonardo da Vinci wrote most of his personal notes in mirror writing. He only used normal writing if he wanted his texts to be read by others. Why he did this is a mystery, but several reasons have been suggested. Friends of Leonardo wrote that they saw him write and paint left handed. Writing left handed in those times was messy because the wet ink would smear as his hand moved across the paper. Writing in reverse would stop it from smudging.

He also could have been using a simple code to make it harder for people to read his notes and steal his ideas. Why do you think Leonardo wrote in reverse?

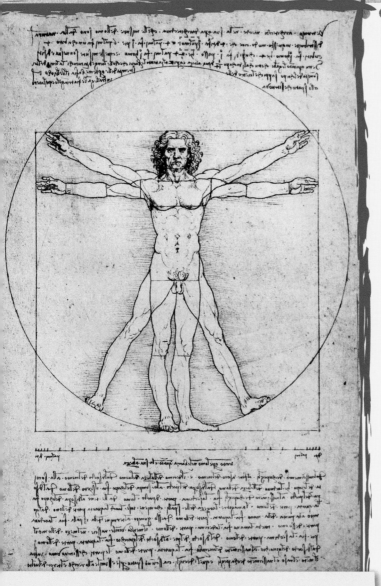

What does it say?

In the red box at the top of the drawing you can see this backward Italian word.

In a mirror it reads like this:

The Italian for palm is "palmo." Leonardo was saying that four fingers was equal to one palm.

Vetruvian Man was drawn by Leonardo based on work by the architect, Vitruvius. It is a perfect blend of art and science. The mirror writing lists the **proportions** of man, for example "the length of outspread arms is equal to the height of a man."

Mona Lisa

Back in Florence, Leonardo painted an artwork that has become one of the most recognized art images in the world, the *Mona Lisa*. For a long time no one knew who the woman was. It is now known that she was Lisa di Gherardini, wife of a Florentine silk trader named Francesco del Giocondo. Leonardo took the painting with him everywhere. After Leonardo died, the painting was given to the king of France, and today, it hangs in the Louvre, a famous museum in Paris.

What's Missing?

There seems to be one thing missing from the *Mona Lisa* portrait. Eyebrows! French engineer Pascal Cotte scanned the *Mona Lisa* with a special camera he invented. The images peel away centuries of varnish to show how she would have appeared to Leonardo when he painted her. A zoomed-in image of Mona Lisa's left eye revealed a single brush stroke in the eyebrow region!

Mona Lisa or
La Gioconda

Anatomist

Leonardo was fascinated by human **anatomy** and spent hours examining **corpses** to figure out how the human body worked. He measured muscles, made diagrams of the organs, and discovered the way blood flows through the body and oxygen fills the lungs. He knew more about the human body than the doctors of his time. Leonardo used this learning in his art. He could draw people in the right proportions and with the right muscle structure.

Leonardo dissected bodies at night, by candlelight. He held a piece of cloth over his mouth and nose to try and get rid of the smell of the corpses. With contagious diseases like the **plague** that were around at the time, this was very risky for his own health. Leonardo was allowed only to dissect dead bodies of criminals.

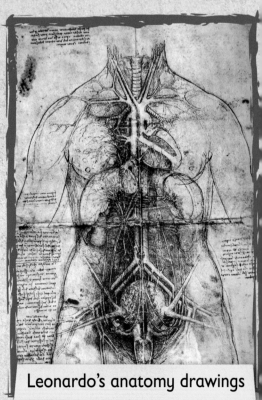

Leonardo's anatomy drawings

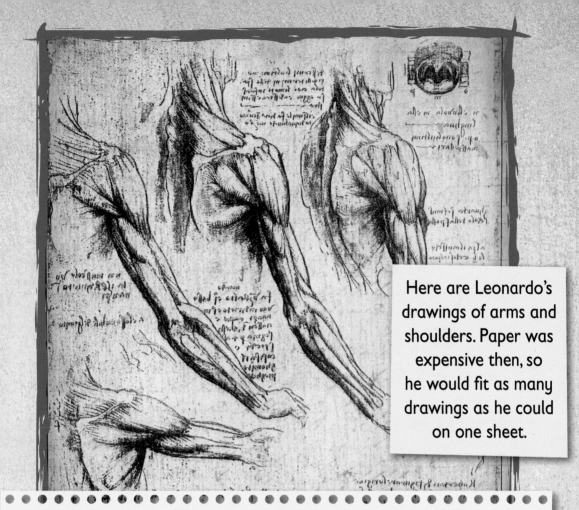

Here are Leonardo's drawings of arms and shoulders. Paper was expensive then, so he would fit as many drawings as he could on one sheet.

Witchcraft and Necromancy!

In 1514, Leonardo was charged with witchcraft and **necromancy**. All of Leonardo's notebooks were analyzed by the **Vatican**. His drawings of bodies, including a child and a pregnant woman, were considered proof of necromancy. His left-handed mirror writing was enough to convict him of witchcraft! Only his talent saved him from being put to death.

Inventor

Leonardo da Vinci was a true "Renaissance man." A Renaissance man is a person with knowledge and skills in many different areas. No one in history has been as accomplished as Leonardo. He drew over 100 inventions in his notebooks. Sadly many of his notebooks are now lost, so we will never know how many more he may have thought up.

Some of his Inventions

- armored tank
- parachute
- life jacket
- scissors
- machine gun
- swing bridge
- submarine
- catapult
- diving suit
- spring driven car
- double hulled boat

Leonardo's study of anatomy meant he understood how muscles moved bone. He used the same principles to build a robot knight. Unlike most of his inventions, Leonardo actually built the robot and used it for entertainment at parties. The robot could walk, sit down, and even move its jaw.

Leonardo's Diving Suit

Leonardo's diving suit was made of leather. The facemask had glass goggles and was connected to a snorkel made of cane. It had a bell that floated on the surface, filled with air. Another version had bladders filled with air, like the tanks we use today. Leonardo was practical, too. The suit included a bottle the diver could go to the bathroom in!

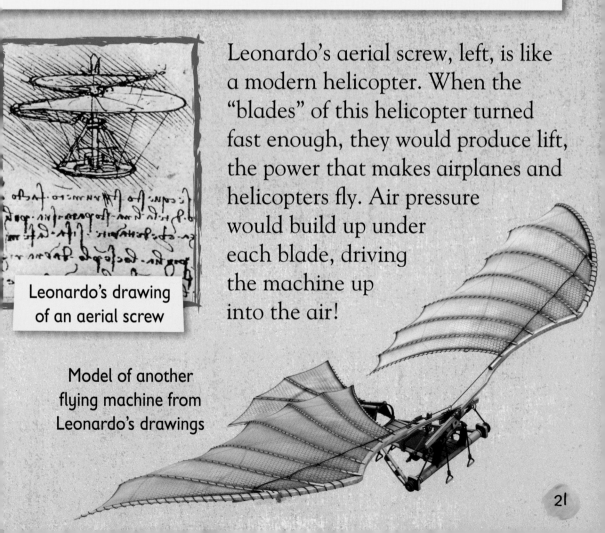

Leonardo's drawing of an aerial screw

Leonardo's aerial screw, left, is like a modern helicopter. When the "blades" of this helicopter turned fast enough, they would produce lift, the power that makes airplanes and helicopters fly. Air pressure would build up under each blade, driving the machine up into the air!

Model of another flying machine from Leonardo's drawings

21

Town Planner

In 1484 the plague struck Milan. Thousands of dead people were left to rot in the streets. Leonardo, being the problem solver that he was, questioned why cities were suffering the spread of disease the worst. He designed a layout of the city with wide streets and canals in place of narrow ones, with sewage disposal, and a system for washing the streets automatically using locks and paddle wheels.

It was a two-story town design, with the top streets for homes and churches, and the bottom streets to be used for deliveries and wagons. The money needed to build such a city were well beyond Leonardo's means, and he never found a **patron** willing to pay to construct it.

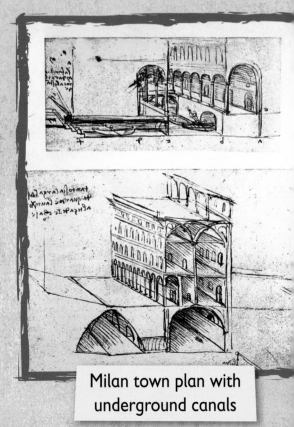

Milan town plan with underground canals

Leonardo designed plans for the perfect horse's stables. His designs even included notes on how to run a fresh, orderly stable. It is thought he based the drawings on the stables at Sforza's castle, Castello Sforzesco, shown in the photo on the right.

The stables at Castello Sforzesco

Patrons

Giuliano de' Medici

Leonardo da Vinci had a number of powerful patrons. Patronage of the arts was important in art history. A patron is a wealthy man who gives support, encouragement, and financial aid to artists. Leonardo's patrons included Francis I, the King of France, the Medici family, Ludovico Sforza, and Cesare Borgia.

The Last Supper

One of Leonardo's most famous paintings is *The Last Supper*. It took him over three years to complete. It was painted for his patron Ludovico Sforza on a wall of the dining hall at the monastery of Santa Maria delle Grazie in Milan, Italy. Some days Leonardo would arrive at sunrise and paint until dark without rest. On other days he would just stand in front of the painting for hours with his arms folded. Sometimes weeks would go by and he wouldn't show up at all.

Restoration

Leonardo da Vinci painted *The Last Supper* on a dry wall rather than on wet plaster like a true fresco. Because of this, the painting began to deteriorate a few years after Leonardo finished it. It has been restored many times.

The Last Supper

The Last Supper shows the reaction of each apostle as Jesus says that one of them will betray him. The apostles are in groups of three. The second group of three from the left are Judas, Peter, and John. Judas is clutching a small bag, perhaps holding the silver given to him as payment to betray Jesus. Some people think John is actually a woman, perhaps Mary Magdalene. What do you think?

Mapmaker

Leonardo became a military engineer for Cesare Borgia, an Italian nobleman from a very powerful family. Leonardo created many maps for his new patron. Leonardo was one of the first **cartographers** to draw maps from a bird's-eye view. Cesare gave Leonardo an unlimited pass to inspect and manage all his construction.

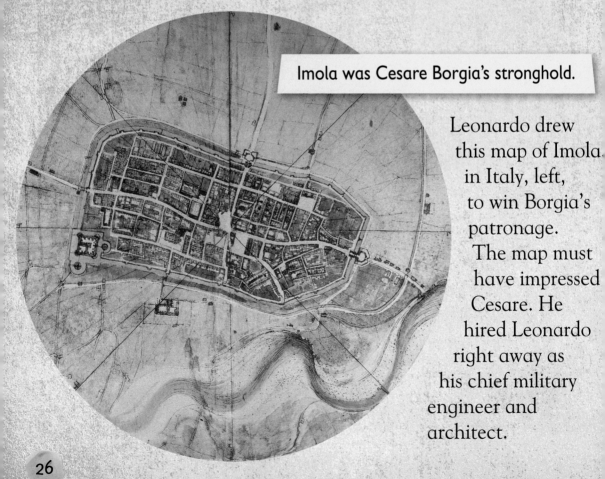

Imola was Cesare Borgia's stronghold.

Leonardo drew this map of Imola in Italy, left, to win Borgia's patronage. The map must have impressed Cesare. He hired Leonardo right away as his chief military engineer and architect.

Cesare Borgia

Cesare Borgia was the ruthless son of Pope Alexander VI. He had a violent reputation and is thought to have killed his own brother, Giovanni. Cesare was killed trying to invade a castle in 1507.

The Rocca of Imola, below, the Sforza Castle, was conquered by Cesare Borgia. He asked Leonardo to figure out how to strengthen the building after the damage suffered by his attack.

Leonardo created many maps for his patron Cesare Borgia. Having a clear idea of the landscape gave Borgia an advantage when waging war. Leonardo recorded all the rivers to give his patron the greatest help possible in battle. Leonardo was the first person known to have used different colors to show how high the mountains were. This information would have helped Borgia plan his attacks, too.

The Last Years

Leonardo left the Borgias after a year and went to Florence, and then Milan. In 1513 he went to Rome, at the invitation of Giuliano de' Medici, who became his patron. In 1516 Medici died, and Leonardo moved to France at the request of King Francis I.

Leonardo moved into a manor house, Clos Lucé, near the royal chateaux in Amboise, France, and became "First Painter and Architect and Engineer of the King." That's some job title!

Did You Know?

Leonardo was a vegetarian all his life. In fact, he was such a devoted vegetarian that he would buy caged chickens and set them free.

Clos Lucé, France, is now a Leonardo da Vinci museum.

Francis I receiving the last breath of Leonardo da Vinci in 1519, by Jean-Auguste-Dominique Ingres.

Leonardo died on May 2, 1519, and legend says he died in the arms of King Francis. Although his paintings are few, he was famous for being a great painter long before his scientific work was acknowledged and appreciated. Five centuries later we still view Leonardo with awe. He was one of the greatest minds ever to have ever lived, and a true "Renaissance man."

Glossary

anatomy
(uh-NA-tuh-mee)
Knowledge of the
structure of an organism.

apprentice
(uh-PREN-tis)
A person learning a trade
or art by working under a
skilled craftsman.

cartographers
(kar-TAH-gruh-furz)
People who make maps.

corpses (KORPS-es)
Dead bodies.

necromancy
(NEH-kruh-mant-see)
The art or practice
of calling up the
spirits of the dead for
magical purposes.

patron (PAY-trun)
One who gives generous
support or approval.

plague (PLAYG)
An epidemic disease
causing a high rate
of death.

proportions
(pruh-POR-shun)
The size of things
compared to the size
of others.

reputation
(reh-pyoo-TAY-shun)
The ideas people have
about another person,
an animal, or an object.

studio (STOO-dee-oh)
A room or building where
an artist works.

tempera (TEM-pur-uh)
A process of painting
in which the colors are
mixed with substances
(as egg, glue, or gum)
other than oil.

Vatican (VA-tih-ken)
The headquarters for
the Pope, leader of the
Roman Catholic church.

Websites

For web resources related to the
subject of this book, go to:
www.windmillbooks.com/weblinks
and select this book's title.

Read More

Bark, Jaspre. *Journal of Inventions: Leonardo da Vinci.* Charlotte, NC: Silver Dolphin Books, 2009.

Nichols, Catherine. *Leonardo da Vinci.* The Primary Source Library of Famous Artists. New York: PowerKids Press, 2006.

Phillips, John. *Leonardo da Vinci: The Genius Who Defined the Renaissance.* World History Biographies. Des Moines, IA: National Geographic Children's Books, 2008.

Index